YOUR KNOWLEDGE HAS VALUE

AF141565

- We will publish your bachelor's and master's thesis, essays and papers

- Your own eBook and book - sold worldwide in all relevant shops

- Earn money with each sale

Upload your text at www.GRIN.com and publish for free

Stefanie Krause

The implementing of the 'Vow of Chastity' in Jan Dunn's "Gypo"

GRIN Verlag

Bibliografische Information der Deutschen Nationalbibliothek:

Die Deutsche Bibliothek verzeichnet diese Publikation in der Deutschen National-
bibliografie; detaillierte bibliografische Daten sind im Internet über http://dnb.d-
nb.de/ abrufbar.

Imprint:

Copyright © 2006 GRIN Verlag GmbH
Druck und Bindung: Books on Demand GmbH, Norderstedt Germany
ISBN: 978-3-638-76811-5

This book at GRIN:

http://www.grin.com/en/e-book/66826/the-implementing-of-the-vow-of-chastity-
in-jan-dunn-s-gypo

GRIN - Your knowledge has value

Der GRIN Verlag publiziert seit 1998 wissenschaftliche Arbeiten von Studenten, Hochschullehrern und anderen Akademikern als eBook und gedrucktes Buch. Die Verlagswebsite www.grin.com ist die ideale Plattform zur Veröffentlichung von Hausarbeiten, Abschlussarbeiten, wissenschaftlichen Aufsätzen, Dissertationen und Fachbüchern.

Visit us on the internet:

http://www.grin.com/

http://www.facebook.com/grincom

http://www.twitter.com/grin_com

Universität Mannheim

Anglistisches Seminar

Hauptseminar: „First films at MA/HD film festival"

WS 2005/06

Hauptseminararbeit:

The implementing of the "Vow of Chastity" in Jan Dunn´s *Gypo*

Stefanie Krause

Magister Artium

<u>Contents</u>

1. Introduction

Gypo is the first UK Dogme95[1]-film, placed on position 37 in the official Dogme-film list[2]. Being produced with a low budget of 250.000 pounds in thirteen days[3], every scene filmed only once and some improvised dialogues without a script for the actors, its international success was a surprise not only for the writer and director Jan Dunn and producer Elaine Whickham. Being invited to numerous film festivals in Europe and the United States it has gained a lot of attention.

The following work will concentrate on the Dogme aspects of *Gypo*. After the introduction, a short overview about *Gypo* will be given in the second chapter. To make it easier to follow the upcoming main analysis in chapter four, this will include a brief summarise of the story. Chapter three concentrate on Dogme itself and its history: how the idea came up, how it developed and which role it has in today's film business. Furthermore it will clarify the religious influences and point out the coherences between *Gypo* and the term Dogme. Chapter four will have the main part. Containing the explanation of the ten Dogme rules – also called the "Vow of Chastity" - it will analyse how they are implemented in Jan Dunn's *Gypo*. These analyses will be added with explanations and comments taken from two different interviews, one by the "Father of Dogme" Lars von Trier[4] to clarify the intentions to make up such rules, and one by Jan Dunn[5] to point up her intention to follow them. In chapter five conclusions will be made concerning the question how Dunn managed to obey the Vow of Chastity. Due to the limited space of this term paper only a few scenes of *Gypo* will be taken out to be analysed more detailed; many scenes that are almost calling for interpretation have to be left aside.

---

[1] In the following text this term will be shortened to "Dogme", which is an official term as well.
[2] No Author. (No date). "Dogme-films". (No update date). http://www.dogme95.dk/menu/menuset.htm. (10.04.2006).
[3] Wood, Sura. (2005). "Gypo.". (2006). San Francisco: The Hollywood Reporter. http://www.hollywoodreporter.com/thr/reviews/review_display.jsp?vnu_content_id=1001021912. (12.04.2006).
[4] Rundle, Peter. (1999). "We are all sinners. Excerpts from an interview given by Lars von Trier." (No update date).http://www.dogme95.dk/news/interview/trier_interview2.htm. (08.04.2006).
[5] Sims, Stella. (2005). "Back to basics. Stella Sims talks to director Elaine Dunn about the challenges involved in making her award-winning debut feature, Gypo, the first certified British Dogme movie.". (No update date). http://www.showreel.org/memberarea/article.php?101. (10.04.2006).

2. *Gypo*

With three well known actors out of five main characters *Gypo*'s cast receives a lot of attention in Britain: Paul McGann as Paul, Pauline McLynn as Helen and Rula Lenska as Irina are all very popular actors or comedians in the UK. Chloe Sirene as Tasha has got several role-offers through her part and will surely make her way, as well as Tamzin Dunstone in the role of Kelly, who was detected at a local theatre.

Like rule number 8 of the Dogme-rules[6] says, *Gypo* does not fit into any kind of genre. It is not even a movie with a single story – it is a movie that tells three stories, depending on the characters perspective. The title is a bad swear word for Romany-Czechs. In short it is a film about a few days in the life of a working-class family living in Margate: Helen, her husband Paul, her daughter Kelly, her granddaughter Jordan, Kelly's schoolmate Tasha and her mother Irina. The marriage of Helen and Paul is not very lucky, as is Helens relationship to her daughter. When her daughter brings in a new "friend" – Tasha, a Czech refugee waiting for her passport - everything changes.

Gypo is told out of three different perspectives: Helen's, Paul's and Tasha's. All three parts are introduced by a sequence at the beach, where the name of the narrating character is laid in the sand with stones and swept away by the waves as a hint that something will change - except Paul's name, that stays static, which might be an allusion to his character being static as well as to his never changing prejudices. Even though Paul does not seem to be a main character as much as Kelly, his perspective is very important to show the view of a slightly racist person. Kelly's view would be very interesting to help understanding how a person develops from a neutral to a right wing conviction, but as she is a teenage girl many of her actions could be blamed to the changing moods of a teenager. Depending on who is "telling" the story, details are left out or emphasized that are not in the other perspectives.

---

[6] See Chapter 4.

3. Dogme95

The third chapter will concentrate on "Dogme95". 3.1 will give a short overview how the idea arised, developed and was dropped again. 3.2 will point out religious influences on Dogme. In 3.3 reasons why *Gypo* is a Dogme-film will be given.

3.1 History of Dogme95

Dogme95 is a manifesto for film production that was brought up by the Danish producers Lars von Trier and Thomas Vinterberg in only 45 minutes. Their intention to do such a manifesto was a kind of protest against the upcoming lack of reality in films, especially in Hollywood productions. Therefore they decided to forbid the manipulation of the film afterwards, for example through special effects or any technical tricks, as well as genre classifications and alienation of time and space in their Vow of Chastity. They were the first ones who signed it. In March 1995 they presented these rules in Paris at the 100th birthday of film, which caused great attention. Von Trier read out the manifesto and afterwards he spread red pamphlets containing the manifesto, then left the room and refused to give any more statements concerning this action when journalists later asked him about it.[7] Three years after the presentation of this manifesto the first films following these rules were presented by Vinterberg and von Trier in Cannes: „The Idiots" and „The Celebration".

Until June 2002, thirty-five Dogme-films have been certificated (two more were up to come, one of them was *Gypo*). As von Trier said in an interview, at this time no perfect Dogme-film has been made and he himself has violated the rules several times in his own films. He admits that it is impossible to follow all of the rules, "like many of the ten commandments of the bible. [...] But the intentions are noble."(von Trier, 1999).

After only two years newly created Dogme-office for certificating Dogme-films had been closed again[8]. The producers decided that they will certificate no more films, because Dogme has almost become a genre on its own - what was not the intention

---

[7] Scheplern, Peter. (No date). "Film According to Dogma Restrictions, obstructions and liberations." (No update date). http://www.dogme95.dk/news/interview/schepelern.htm. (10.04.2006).
[9] Nielsen-Ourö, David & Rørsgaard , Ann-sofie. (2002). „The Dogmesecretariat is closing." (No update date). http://www.dogme95.dk/news/interview/pressemeddelelse.htm. (10.04.2006).

when composing the manifesto. They also felt cheated when other persons than directors applied for the certificate, because only the director of a film can decide if he intended to do a Dogme-film. Another reason for closing the office was the fact that it seems impossible to keep all rules, like the committee has experienced in its own projects. They saw it more as a question of conscience if a director feels he or she has abided by the rules or not, and additionally this would be judged by the audience who watches the film. In addition to that they do not have any more economic foundation to continue with their work, partly also because they have – after ten years of Dogme-films - moved on to new experimental film projects.

Instead of going on with certifying or regretting certifications, they choose that everyone who wants to shoot a Dogme-film can feel free to follow the rules and to publish the result, the list of films will be continued in the internet. The group officially split in March 2005.[9]

3.2. The religious aspect in Dogme95

The Vow of Chastity is not only a religious vow as von Trier admits (von Trier, 1999). But this analogy was intended as the fact shows, that he compared the whole idea with the holy rules and called himself a sinner because he does not keep the rules. The producers who intend to make a Dogme-film have to swear to abide the rules as well as members of a religious group have to if they want to join it. He also compared the change in the approval procedure to converting from Catholicism to Protestantism. Of course also the term Dogme itself is a hint to the connection of his rules to religious aspects, as well as the number of the rules: exactly as many as the ten commandments in the bible. The contrast between the ways how Dogme and Hollywood films are produced reminds at the fight between good and evil- that Hollywood is not portrayed as the holly one here is obvious. The last vow that is not count by number – maybe to keep the number of rules equal to those of the commandments, maybe to highlight it in a special way – emphasizes how many constrictions a producer has to accept to be taken in into the small group of chosen ones – definitely an ironic allusion to the religious cult.

---

[9] Wunderlich, Dieter. (2005). "Dogma 95." (2005). http://www.dieterwunderlich.de/dogma_95_film.htm. (10.04.2006).

3.3 *Gypo* and Dogme95

How does a director come to the idea to shoot a Dogme-film and force him - or (like in Dunn's case) herself - to follow ten rules that were set up ten years ago by four Danish producers, instead of filming without any restrictions?

When Jan Dunn and Elaine Wickham met through a new talents initiative, Dunn suggested writing a story containing the local contentious asylum-seeking issues. She wanted to produce it after the Dogme rules if it was to be a gritty, social-based drama, because she thought this would suit to Dogme and that it would be useful for the themes they were exploring. It should become quite raw and should be filmed with a hand-held camera, the realistic impression should be won by avoiding technical finesses and special effects and by using a naturally given environment instead of artificially sets and added props. Wickham as a big Dogme-fan agreed immediately and a few weeks later they met the Dogme advisor Nielsen in Copenhagen who told them, that it would be the first UK Dogme-film. Even though it was sometimes very hard not to break up the Vow of Chastity, they managed with little exceptions to follow the rules. After finishing the film, Dunn says that it was "creatively liberating", but that she will never shoot a Dogme-film again (Dunn, 2005), so it seems that it has more difficulties than advantages to swear the Vow of Chastity.

Being placed on position 37 on the Dogme-list, *Gypo* is the last officially certificated Dogme-film. The office has been closed while the shooting was in planning and the producers decided to give no more certifications; therefore *Gypo* plays a special role in the Dogme-history. Followed by three more British films it has a kind of precursor position.

4. The "Vow of Chastity" in *Gypo*

In the following chapter the ten Dogme rules will be set up, explained and it will be worked out how Dunn follows them in *Gypo*.

4.1 Dogme-rule #1: "Shooting must be done on location. Props and sets must not be brought in (if a particular prop is necessary for the story, a location must be chosen where this prop is to be found)."

Dunn chooses Margate as location; the portrayal of this city is exactly like it looks in reality. The chosen locations like the house of Helen's family, the trailer park, the harbour, the streets, the bar and the hotel really do exist in the form they are shown in the film. The fact that all the locations are not far away from each other does not only give the impression that the inhabitants live in their own narrow world, but is also a hint that some of them are narrow-minded, too - especially Paul, even though he is in the end the only one who managed to escape from this scenery.

That props must not be brought in makes it for a Christmas scenery necessary to shoot around Christmas time. This has been done in *Gypo* - there is Christmas decoration in the streets, a Christmas tree is in the living room, the Margate Christmas procession takes place at that time, the bar is adorned and even Paul's car is decorated with Christmas stuff. Even though the decoration of the car was not originally in there before, Dunn did not break up the rules. She uses a "trick" to make it fit: the crew did the decoration with props from the hotel where they stayed – and therefore it was available at the location and does not hurt the rule. But she hurts the rule in the scene with the blow job. She brought in a prosthetic penis, because she did not want to ask Paul McGann if he would offer his real one for this scene (Dunn, 2005) and therefore took an artificial one, which is definitely a prop. Maybe she could have shoot it from a slightly different perspective, that one could not see it and therefore it would not have been necessary to bring it in and to hurt the rule.

Von Trier explained that the rule is meant in that way, that reality and not fiction should be filmed. If a certain prop in a house is necessary for the shooting but is missing, a house has to be found where the prop is already inside, because it would not be reality anymore if it would be added afterwards (von Trier, 1999). This rule is meant to avoid fictional elements. For example, a Dogme-film could not contain aliens, because there will be no location where they naturally appear and therefore they would have to be brought in, what is against the rules.

4.2 Dogme-rule #2: "The sound must never be produced apart from the images or vice versa. (Music must not be used unless it occurs where the scene is being shot)."

Sounds are only allowed when they occur in the image. This rules leads to a quite bothered viewing of the film, because nowadays one is used to watch films or series underlined by effects or music. The fact that films even got Oscars or other prices for their soundtracks evokes the conclusion that this is an important part of the film, as well as the actors or the action. It helps creating suspense or to strengthen the surprise effect by underlining the action and demanding more than one sense. Scenes with music are affecting the eyes and the ears, while Dogme-films requiring more the visual sense and the concentration on the actual action and not the one that might come up like in Hollywood films, where the surprise moment is introduced by thrilling music before it really comes in. Therefore Dogme-films are not only more focused on the present action but are also less foreseeing, because the viewer has to think for himself what could happen next instead of simply interpreting the music that makes him aware that he has to be attentive because it introduces something upcoming. But all in all *Gypo* – with little exceptions - does well without additional music, even though it is irritating a little bit if you are not aware of the second Dogme-rule when watching the film for the first time: you have the feeling something is missing but you do not know exactly what.

Especially the scenes taking place at the sea seem to be extremely silent - compared with ocean scenes from other films where the sound is much louder - it gives the impression that the sea is farer away because it is so silent, although it is the realistic volume at this distance.

A sequence in which one becomes really aware of how much one is nowadays influenced by soundtracks is when Tasha flees from her husband at the ferry station. The thrilling music that usually creates or strengthened the suspensful effect is missing, so that this scene seems less exciting compared with other films where chasing-scenes are underlined with fast music.

Another scene that usually would have been joined by music is when Helen arrives at the ferry station and finds out that she is too late to help Tasha and Irina. Her helplessness and distraught could have been supported by a disorientating music, but Dunn did her best in keeping to the rules by turning the camera around Helen furiously so that it seems that she does not know where to go and that nothing makes sense anymore, without the assistance of dizzying music.

When Paul enters the bar, the background music seems to silent for this surrounding, too, because a bar is expected to be loud, but only very little and silent music and some sounds of a billiard game can be heard. Usually scenes in bars are underlined with loud music, talking people, and clinking glasses; therefore this scene seems quite unusual and too silent to be realistic.

A further sequence where music appears is in Paul's car when he is listening to a football game on the radio. Here the sound is during the first seconds present at the place of shooting – in his car - and so does not hurt the rules. But in the second shot the car is shown rolling down the street in an extreme long shot, here the sound must have been produced apart from the image, because the car is too far away from the camera that the radio can be heard - even the sound of the engine could not be heard from this distance.

The scene where Helen and Tasha go to the Margate Christmas procession is joined by the sound of the procession. When the two women are shown in an long shot the music appears to be louder than it would be in reality because it is as loud as if the camera were inside the action - like in the next sequence. Therefore it can be assumed that the sound in the first sequence was recorded at the same place where the second sequence took place and hence was produced apart from the image.

Lars von Trier compared shooting a Dogme-film with shooting the first talk movies, because at that time it was not possible to add the sound afterwards - like it should be in a Dogme-film as well. Producing a Dogme-film should be a movement from the modern ways and possibilities back to the basics of producing. Therefore much more planning in advance has to be done by the producer because nothing should be changed or added afterwards.

What might be a big disadvantage of this rule is the fact that it is not allowed to synchronise a Dogme-film into another language, because then the sound would be produced apart from the image. But watching a film that is very hard to follow through the handheld camera and "lower" quality like in *Gypo* would not be fun anymore if you have additionally to concentrate on the subtitles because the film is in a foreign language, for example Danish or Swedish.

4.3 Dogme-rule #3: "The camera must be hand-held. Any movement or immobility attainable in the hand is permitted. (The film must not take place where the camera is standing; shooting must take place where the film takes place)."

Another rule that makes the whole movie seem more realistic is the one, that the camera must be hand-held. Therefore the viewer feels deeper involved in the action, as if he is seeing the whole scenery through his own eyes instead of through a camera. It reminds a bit at Aristoteles' unities of time and place, no flashbacks or foreseeings are allowed and the action has to be recorded where and when it takes place.

Von Trier interpreted the rule together with rule number nine - which says a 35mm camera should be used - in that way, that such a camera is usually shoulder mounted. He and the other Dogme-inventors constructed shoulder mounts for their cameras, so that they do not held the cameras in their hands, like the rule asks for, but somewhere else attached to their bodies (von Trier, 1999). If the rule is interpreted in this way, *Gypo* does confirm the rule permanently because in the chasing-scene the camera is attached to Tasha's body and is therefore not static but where the action takes places. This was probably the best way to shoot this scene, because if the camera was not attached to Tasha or someone who is following her, the shooting would not have taken place where the action did and so it would not confirmed to the rule. This technique also makes the viewer more aware of the fact how frantically Tasha is because everything surrounding her is shaking and cannot really be focused, so the viewer experiences at his own senses how Tasha must feel at this moment. So one concentrates on her facial expression which is desperate and one feels more involved in the action; this is a little "substitute" for the missing thrilling music and creates suspense as well.

Filming with a hand-held camera mainly creates the effect of a point-of-view-shot, this becomes obvious when Helen is at the ferry station, looking around helplessly, not knowing where to go, here the camera turns around as well as Helen does. When Helen knocks on the door of the trailer, we see through Irina's view that she is standing in front of the door and this is reinforced through the fact that we hear Irina speaking ("It's Helen.").

If the camera should be attached to the cameraman or to one of the actors is not mentioned, and so Dunn has done well in interpreting the rule within the limits of the Vow of Chastity.

4.4 Dogme-rule #4: "The film must be in colour. Special lighting is not acceptable. (If there is too little light for exposure the scene must be cut or a single lamp be attached to the camera)."

As well as artificial sounds are forbidden, artificial lighting must not occur as well. The result of this is that the film is coloured in the same tone as it would be in reality and not in special tones, brightened or darkened. If the lighting is not sufficient for a scene, a small lamp attached to the camera is allowed. If the scenery is too dark to film even with such a small lamp it must be shoot in any other way, at any other time or at any other place, or be left out completely, because it is not allowed to make the scenery visible through the usage of infra-red lights.

As Lars von Trier confesses, this rule was made up for himself, because he has "always felt it difficult to accept the way a colour film looks"[10]. He was sad of always spending so much time and energy in changing it afterwards that he decided to make up this rule. He states this with a good argument: "There are things that you simply can't do, so you don't have to worry about them."(von Trier, 1999).

Dunn complained in an interview that this rule caused problems in one particular scene, the one with the blow job, which has to be shoot at night to be realistic (no one would visit a prostitute at the street corner in daylight were everyone could see him). Therefore Paul had to park his car under a street lamp where the prostitute was waiting. Because this one and the interior lamp were not bright enough, Dunn tried a small lamp that was attached to the camera (what is confirm to the rules). This looked at first like floodlight, so it was dimmed afterwards that it looked again like it was night (Dunn, 2005): So far the shooting itself does not hurt the rules. But the fact that the lamp was

---

[10] We are all sinners. By Peter Rundle. Lars von Trier in his office, Wednesday November 4th 1999.

dimmed afterwards and not before or during the shooting seems to be a violation and will be explained more detailed in point 4.5.

4.5 Dogme-rule #5: "Optical work and filters are forbidden."

Filters and optical work are forbidden, so the natural colours stay real and details could not be emphasized by the use of special colouring. These rules - as well as rules two, three and four - give *Gypo* the impression that it is a documentary. Everything is shown just the way it is in reality and therefore it seems to be the pure truth. Dunn seems to abide this rule in exception of one scene: the blow job scene. Here the light that was attached to the camera was dimmed afterwards as she confesses. This can be compared to a filter that is added afterwards. If the lamp had been dimmed before or during the shooting it would have been allowed, but to change the recordings afterwards is optical work and therefore forbidden. To avoid this, the ninth rule prescribed the film format: Von Trier argues that a film is more difficult to manipulate (what a dimming afterwards definitely is) than a video (von Trier, 1999).

4.6 Dogme-rule #6: "The film must not contain superficial action. (Murders, weapons, etc. must not occur.)"

As superficial actions like murders or weapons are forbidden, Dunn has to use different techniques to make the scene when Tasha and her mother are attacked by a gang appearing more dramatic. Their spreading over with Ketchup from their chips has the same optical effect on Helen when she meets them – she is scared and worried about them – as it would have had with real blood, but it is not superficial in this case. The action that leads to their scary outlooking could have been caused by superficial action like Tasha or Irina being attacked brutality with weapons or even been killed, but for Dunn it was sufficient enough for the story line to keep the attack almost harmless with some hustling. Anyway, the manner it was done is excellent, because the viewer believes that something really awful has happened to both of the refugees until it reveals in the last of the three parts that it was only Ketchup and they were indeed treated badly, but not as bad as it seems at first when they came down the street and met Helen. Even if it had been as it looked in the beginning – like weapons were used – it would be interpretation if it were confirming to the rules as long as the action itself is not shown.

4.7 Dogme-rule #7: "Temporal and geographical alienation are forbidden. (That is to say that the film takes place here and now.)"

Here Dunn uses a special technique to avoid back- and forward movements in time. She simply tells the story out of three different perspectives. By making the story look like a detective story through giving the viewers only piece by piece the needed information, without using flashbacks, the continuity of time is given. Each of the three parts is a story of its own and so it is no flashback if the same scene happens again but slightly different. So it has the same effect like a flashback in a detective story: during the second and the third watching more and more details, that did not get that much attention during the first watching, become obvious now when one sees it again. To allow the viewer an orientation where he is temporally placed, in each of the three perspectives certain elements and actions are repeated.

4.8 Dogme-rule #8: "Genre movies are not acceptable."

This rule was brought up to keep the suspense before and during the movie. If one is going to watch a genre movie one knows what could be expected, for example in a love story there have to be lovers - or at least one person who is in love -, in a western there have to be cowboys, horses, great landscapes, thieves, bars, barmaids, Indians and duels. One is expecting certain features and would be irritated if some were missing: a western without a lonely hero would certainly cause confusion in the audience. Also are there some "restrictions" concerning the storyline of a genre. For example if Aliens were trying to conquer the world in a love story it would certainly be seen as a humorous addition but not as an earnest part of the action, or the whole film would be considered as a comedy and therefore "love story" would not be the genre but a part of the movie.

Dunn's *Gypo* does not fit into any genre. It may have similarities with already existing genres but has too many different elements to classify it. It could be a drama, a documentary about British social class workers and the labour market, a social critical film that wants to inform about the problematic of teenage pregnancy, a film about refugees and prejudices about them, a biography of a variety of British citizens that accidentally have a close connection to each other, a kind of detective story where the viewer has to find out how that happens what he sees in the first part, a story of failed love and domestic violence, it could also be a homosexual love story. There are many possibilities to name contained features, but it is impossible to name one particular genre in which *Gypo* takes its place, therefore each viewer will have different expectations to this film.

4.9 Dogme-rule #9: "The film format must be Academy 35 mm."

This rule has lead to some confusion between the producers who brought it up and they discussed very intensively if this format has to be for shooting as well as for the distribution. They decided that a producer can choose how he or she shoots the film as long as it is distributed in the compulsory format, so that the cameraman does not have to carry a heavy 35 mm camera all the time. The fact that the shooting itself can be also done on video has lead to the trend that many cheap Dogme-films have been produced – films that maybe would not have been produced if this rule would have prescribed the usage of an expensive camera. The first intention to make up this rule was, that it is much easier to manipulate a video-format than a film-format and that manipulation (for example the changing of the colour grade) should be avoided, which was the main idea of the whole manifesto. *Gypo* has the required format, but as no information about how it was shoot could be found, it must be assumed that this rule has less importance for the film itself than the other ten ones.

4.10 Dogme-rule #10: "The director must not be credited."

The last rule was more a joke and a provocation than serious meant, as von Trier said in an interview (von Trier, 1999). The intention to develope it was to show that the film itself should be more important than the name that stands after it, as a hint that many Hollywood films get more attention when they were directed by a big name instead of a "nobody", independent of the film and its story itself. This nuisance should be erased through the fact that the director must not be credited and therefore could not be discussed. Von Trier thinks the film is more important than the one who made it and he felt this idea "quite noble. [...] It's about seeking some form of truth - that this truth is more important than whatever honour it might give you later."(von Trier, 1999). He was aware of the fact that many directors will not accept this rule – like he himself: he is always credited in his films!

In the prefix of *Gypo* only the production companies (Medb Films, DistantEye Films and Spotty Dog Films) and the five main actors are credited. This happens – as rule two says, without afterwards added sound, what is quite disturbing, because being introduced into a film is in most cases joined with music that takes you into the actual mood of the opening scene. In the trailer Dunn broke the rule: here she is mentioned as producer.

4.11 Final declaration: "Furthermore I swear as a director to refrain from personal taste! I am no longer an artist. I swear to refrain from creating a "work", as I regard the instant as more important than the whole. My supreme goal is to force the truth out of my characters and settings. I swear to do so by all the means available and at the cost of any good taste and any aesthetic considerations. Thus I make my Vow of Chastity."

This is the final statement of the Vow of Chastity, which evokes the suspicion that the producers want to make one last try to avoid that everybody starts to shoot Dogme-films without occupying with the idea that stands after all these rules. The intensity with which they demand the abidance of the Vow of Chastity makes the whole manifesto a ridiculous joke that cannot be taken too serious by anyone.

5. Conclusion

Summed up I can say that Dunn has done her job very well. She has tried to follow the rules wherever it was possible and where it was not, she has tried to work with tricks to avoid breaking them. Even though this has not worked sometimes, those scenes are so less that in general it can be said that *Gypo* has earned the term Dogme-film. The violation of the rules are acceptable, because the "inventor" of Dogme itself, Lars von Trier, has confessed that it is impossible to follow all the rules, like it is impossible to follow the ten commandments and therefore I think Dunn has really done great in hurting the rules so seldom.

What I think impairs the joy of watching a little bit is that the unusual and amateurish camerawork and the way how some scenes are shot makes the watching pretty exhausting. I would not recommend this film for relaxing after a hard day, but as a movie one has to think and maybe discuss about with somebody afterwards. Surely Dunn does not intend to make a purely entertaining film but one people think of afterwards, otherwise she would not have taken such explosive topics like teenage pregnancy, violence and prejudices against immigrants, family violence and other social problems. But other Dogme-films have proved already that even with following the rules a Dogme-film does not have to be that stressful to follow and does not even have to be recognised as such, because excellent and professional camera work is not excluded by the rules.

6. Bibliography

Benyahia, Sarah Casey. (2005). *Teaching contemporary British cinema*. Great Britain: Cromwell Press Ltd.

Buckland, Warren. (1998). *Film Studies. Teach yourself*. London: Hodder & Stoughton.

Corrigan, Timothy. ([5]2004). *A short guide to writing about film*. New York: Longman.

Dunn, Jan: Gypo. UK 2005. available at http://www.swipefilms.com/. (12.04.2006).

Hayward, Susan. ([2]2003). *Cinema Studies. The key concepts*. Bury St. Edmunds, Suffolk: St. Edmundsbury Press Ltd.

Higson, Andrew. (1995). *Waving the flag: constructing a national Cinema in Britain*. Oxford: Clarendon Press.

Hollows, Joanne & Hutchings, Peter & Janovich, Mark (Ed.). (2000). *The film studies reader*. London: Arnold.

Medb films. (No date). Gypo. http://www.gypothefilm.co.uk/. (06.04.2006).

No Author. (No date). "Dogme-films". (No update date). http://www.dogme95.dk/menu/menuset.htm. (06.04.2006).

Park, James. (1990). *British cinema. The light that failed*. London. D.T. Batsford Ltd.

Rundle, Peter. (4.11.1999). "We are all sinners. Excerpts from an interview given by Lars von Trier." (No update date). http://www.dogme95.dk/news/interview/trier_interview2.htm. (08.04.2006).

Sargeant; Amy. ([3]1996). "Marking out the territory: aspects of British cinema." In: Nelmes, Jill (Ed.). *An Introduction to Film Studies*. London: Routledge, 321-358.

Scheplern, Peter. (No date). "Film According to Dogma Restrictions, obstructions and liberations." (No update date). http://www.dogme95.dk/news/interview/schepelern.htm. (10.04.2006).

Sims, Stella. (2005). "Back to basics. Stella Sims talks to director Elaine Dunn about the challenges involved in making her award-winning debut feature, Gypo, the first certified British Dogme movie.". (No update date). http://www.showreel.org/memberarea/article.php?101. (10.04.2006).

Wood, Sura. (2005). "Gypo.". (2006). San Francisco: The Hollywood Reporter. http://www.hollywoodreporter.com/thr/reviews/review_display.jsp?vnu_content_id=10 01021912. (12.04.2006).

Wunderlich, Dieter. (2005). "Dogma 95." (2005). http://www.dieterwunderlich.de/dogma_95_film.htm. (10.04.2006).